HALF HUMAN HALF MACHINE

EQUIPPING MANAGERS FOR THE AI REVOLUTION

NIKHIL RAJ NATARAJAN

Made with ♥ on the Notion Press Platform
www.notionpress.com

To my beloved family, whose unwavering support has been the foundation upon which I stand

- To my parents, V.Natarajan and Lalitha Bai, Mani Gopalan and Suseela, your love, guidance, and belief in me have fuelled my journey every step of the way.
- To my wife, Simi, your love, understanding, and encouragement have been the constant wind beneath my wings. Thank you for your unwavering support, for celebrating my achievements, and for being my partner in all things.
- To my siblings, Nithin Raj Natarajan and Vidhya K Vijayan, Mithun and Chinnu, Smitha and Shyam, your friendship and support mean the world to me. Thank you for always having my back.
- To my wonderful children, Niyah Nikhil, Nila Nikhil, Nivin Raj, Nadhav Raj, Mihika and Rana, your inquisitive minds and boundless curiosity inspire me every day. May this book serve as a testament to the power of learning and the importance of pursuing your dreams.

And to my esteemed mentors, Leen B. Jesmas, R.Sreekandan Nair, Joseph CT, Sabu Shumsudeen and Joseph Ignatius, friends and well wishers, your invaluable guidance and mentorship have shaped my path and nurtured my growth. Thank you.
I also extend my sincere gratitude to Tata Elxsi for providing me with exceptional training in Artificial Intelligence and the invaluable opportunities to practice and apply my newfound knowledge.
Above all, I thank God for the blessings, strength, and guidance that have made this journey possible.

This book is dedicated to all of you, with heartfelt gratitude.

Contents

Preface

Welcome to "Half Human Half Machine." In an era defined by rapid technological advancements and the blurring of boundaries between humans and machines, the intersection of humanity and artificial intelligence (AI) has become increasingly complex and intriguing. This book explores the multifaceted relationship between humans and machines, offering insights into the profound implications of this evolving symbiosis.

As the author of "Half Human Half Machine," I have been captivated by the transformative potential of AI and its impact on our society, economy, and individual lives. Through this book, I aim to delve into the nuances of this dynamic relationship, shedding light on the challenges, opportunities, and ethical considerations that arise as humans and machines become increasingly intertwined.

My goal in writing this book is to empower leaders, managers, and decision-makers with the knowledge and tools they need to harness the full potential of AI in their organizations. Whether you are a seasoned executive leading a digital transformation initiative or a manager seeking to leverage AI to drive performance improvements, "Half Human, Half Machine" offers valuable insights and practical case studies to help you succeed in the age of intelligent automation.

As you embark on this journey through the world of AI in business, I encourage you to approach each chapter with curiosity and an open mind. Together, let us embrace the opportunities that AI presents and chart a course towards a future where humans and machines work together in harmony to achieve extraordinary results.

Turn the page and let's begin!

Nikhil Raj Natarajan

I

Understanding the Role of AI in Business

In today's rapidly evolving, tech-driven business landscape, staying ahead of the curve is crucial for business success. This is where Artificial Intelligence (AI) emerges as a powerful tool for managers seeking to elevate their performance and propel their organizations forward. This book delves deep into the world of AI from a manager's perspective, providing a comprehensive guide on how to leverage its capabilities to enhance decision-making and ultimately drive performance improvements.

The book begins by breaking down complex AI concepts into simple, easy-to-understand language, ensuring accessibility even for those with limited technical expertise. Through compelling real-world examples and case studies, readers gain valuable insights into how AI is revolutionizing diverse industries, from media and healthcare to customer service and manufacturing.

Moving forward, the book empowers managers to become active participants in the AI revolution within their own organizations. It equips them with the knowledge and tools to identify specific opportunities where AI can be utilized to optimize processes, improve efficiency, and ultimately enhance decision-making across various departments. Tailored to address real-world managerial challenges, the book presents practical use cases that demonstrate the potential applications of AI in various scenarios.

Furthermore, the book takes a strategic approach to AI implementation, guiding managers in developing clear and actionable frameworks for integrating AI into their organizations. It emphasizes ethical considerations and potential biases, ensuring responsible and transparent AI adoption. Additionally, it equips managers with the skills necessary to manage and evaluate the performance of AI systems, maximizing their impact and ensuring optimal results.

Moving beyond just using AI, this book empowers managers to become leaders in shaping their organization's future through the intelligent application of this powerful technology. It equips them with the knowledge and skills to navigate common challenges, such as addressing employee concerns and navigating cultural shifts associated with AI implementation. By fostering collaboration and a culture of innovation, managers are better equipped to lead their teams towards a future powered by AI.

This book is more than just a guide; it's a transformational toolkit that equips managers and leaders to leverage AI effectively, unlock its potential, and ultimately drive success in their organizations.

AI-Driven Project Management

AI has changed project management to a large extent by providing capabilities to deal with complex tasks and adapt to dynamic environments. AI streamlines process, enhances efficiency, and contributes to overall business success. It empowers to make informed decisions, implement AI solutions effectively, and become a leader in the age of intelligent automation.

Implementing AI-powered project management software with advanced features such as automated scheduling, intelligent resources management, and real-time progress tracking is important at this stage. Such tools helps for performance improvement, elimination of mistakes, and agile decision-making which in turn translates into a successful implementation of the project . AI programs can use big data and analyse to find possible risks and come up with the best mitigation strategies. Thus, the preventive approach enables project Managers to mitigate the risks, to minimize possible disruptions and to ensure project completion as expected.

AI algorithms helps to optimize resource allocation, ensuring the right resources are allocated at the right time and in the right quantity. This results in improved resource utilization, cost savings, and timely project completion. AI-powered quality assurance and testing platforms automate processes, detect defects, and provide insights to enhance project quality. These platforms reduce time-to-market and ensure superior product quality.

AI automates financial processes, optimizes budget allocation, and provides real-time financial insights. This empowers Project Managers to make informed financial decisions, track expenses, and ensure financial success. AI algorithms enable real-time performance monitoring, data analysis, and automated reporting. Project Managers gain valuable insights to optimize project performance.

AI-powered platforms enhance team collaboration, automate tasks, and improve communication efficiency, encouraging seamless project coordination.

AI-based tools automate change impact analysis, stakeholder engagement and communication, facilitating successful navigation of organizational changes.

AI-driven predictive analytics tools enable accurate forecasting of project outcomes based on historical data and trends. This data-driven approach allows managers to make informed decisions, mitigate risks, and ensure successful project completion.

In conclusion, AI has emerged as a game-changer for IT Project Managers. By embracing AI technologies and leveraging the various AI-driven tools and solutions available, Project Managers can optimize processes, enhance decision-making capabilities, mitigate risks, and achieve successful project outcomes. . The AI acceptance is no longer a matter of choice or preference, but the necessity for any Project / Program / Portfolio Manager who wants to stay updated or competitive in the fast developing business environment.

The author of this book is managing a Portfolio of accounts with a track record of successfully managing highly complex programs. He is working for Tata Elxsi Limited during the time he penned it down. He has effectively used GEN AI tools to write this book , which serves as a curated guide for the Business leaders about AI and demonstrating how seamlessly projects can be managed with Artificial Intelligence.

Given that this book primarily caters to managers, it includes only brief summaries of topics. For more comprehensive details about any of the listed subjects, kindly refer to the internet.

Challenges and Limitations of AI in Project Management

Artificial intelligence excels in streamlining processes, enhancing efficiency, and improving decision-making. However, it is important to acknowledge that AI is not a one-size-fits-all solution and there are challenges and limitations that need to be considered when implementing AI in Project Management.

One of the key challenges is the complexity of integrating AI into existing systems and processes. AI-driven project management software, risk assessment and mitigation tools, resource allocation and optimization solutions, and other AI-based tools require compatibility with existing IT infrastructure. This can be a significant challenge, especially for organizations with legacy systems or limited technical capabilities. It is crucial to ensure that proper integration and interoperability measures are in place to maximize the benefits of AI.

Another limitation of AI in Project Management is the need for high-quality, accurate data. AI algorithms rely on data to learn and make predictions, and if the data is incomplete, inconsistent, or biased, it can lead to flawed outcomes. Project Managers should invest in data quality management and data governance processes to ensure that the data made available for the AI system is reliable and unbiased.

AI also has limitations when it comes to complex decision-making. While AI-based decision support systems can provide valuable insights and recommendations, the final decision still rests with the Project Manager. It is important to strike a balance between relying on AI recommendations and leveraging human judgment and expertise.

While AI offers immense potential in Project Management, it is important to recognize and address the challenges and limitations that come with it. By understanding and mitigating these challenges, IT Project Managers can maximize the benefits of AI and make smarter decisions for successful Project execution.

II

Industry 4.0

The new industrial era, known as Industry 4.0 or the 4th Industrial Revolution, marks the fourth stage of the digital transformation of the manufacturing and distribution processes for companies worldwide. Businesses are adopting a range of modern technologies, including IoT, cloud systems, analytics, and AI, which smartly connects to their operations and production processes, facilitating the digitalization of business activities.

Such new facilities, which can be called smart factories, incorporate advanced sensors, embedded software and robotics into the gathering and analysing of data which give room for informed decision making. With convergence of data from different sources like production, ERP, supply chain, and CRM integration, there arises the visibility and insight previously unheard of as compared to traditional data silos.

The creation of smart factories will offer the manufacturing sector the capability to exploit the immense potential of big data. Real time monitoring of machines with the help of sensor data will lead to optimal working and hence predictive maintenance strategies will be taken to reduce machines breakdown to minimum.

Utilizing the most modern IoT devices in smart factories is a way to boost productivity and nurture consistent product quality. AI-run visual inspection systems do the work that was manually done, so it cuts down the errors and saves both time and money. Through this approach, resource costs can be kept down even as remote employees are able to use their cloud-connected smartphones to view processes under monitoring at any time.

With the help of machine learning algorithms manufacturers can quickly locate and fix errors much sooner than later in production schedules, thus avoiding undesired setbacks. The concepts and skills of Industry 4.0 are universal and can be used in different business domains.

Steam to Sensor

The progression of industrial revolutions is notable: the first revolution was propelled by steam, the second one by electricity, the third was preliminary automation with machinery while the current one is controlled by cyber-physical systems which are also known as artificial intelligence.

INDUSTRY 1.0	INDUSTRY 2.0	INDUSTRY 3.0	INDUSTRY 4.0
Mechanization	Electrification	Automation	Cyber-physical systems
Mechanization of production using Steam & Water Power	Labour Based Mass production using Electrical Energy	Automated Production, Computers , IT Systems and Robotics	Convergence of Physical, digital and virtual , Cyber Physical Systems, Machine Learning & IoT

First industrial revolution began in the late 18th century marked the achievement of mass production with the mere use of water and steam power which replaced human and animal labour. Machinery was in replacement for handcrafts; thus production techniques were revolutionized.

In the next century, the second industrial revolution has led to mass production through the use of assembly lines and the consumption of oil, gas, and electricity. These energy sources, along with telephone and telegraph for communication, contributed to the production of mass and automated machines to a certain degree.

The third industrial revolution, which appeared in the middle of the 20th century, mixed computers, modern telecommunications, and data analysis together for industrial purposes. Factories first went digital by introducing programmable logic controllers (PLCs), which were gradually incorporated into machinery, thereby standardizing the production processes and enabling both data collection and sharing.

Now we are in the fourth industrial revolution, the age of increased computerization and an implantation of the smart robots & smart enterprises. Data analytics helps in making informed decisions and thus improves efficiency and productivity at the value chain level. Flexibility is designed into the whole system so that even a large size of one product can be produced efficiently. By coupling data from the floor with enterprise operational information, the smart factory optimizes information transparency to provide better decision-making.

III

Artificial Intelligence

Artificial intelligence (AI) is the imitation of the human behaviour of thinking, reasoning, and learning by a machine, especially computer systems. These processes comprise of thinking, reasoning, solving problems, understanding language, perception ability, and making decisions. AI gives machines the ability to execute activities that require human intelligence, like recognizing patterns in data, comprehending natural language, and making valid assumptions based on past events.

AI systems are programmed to process huge chunks of data, identify patterns and trends and finally make decisions using the data analysis. Machine learning algorithms can be trained using labelled data sets, where the algorithm rips the patterns from given examples by humans.

AI has a number of subfields, such as machine learning, natural language processing, computer vision, robotics and expert systems. Machine learning, in particular, is a branch of AI that focuses on enabling machines to learn from data without prior programming. This is done by means of the algorithms that are constantly refined as they are exposed the more and more data.

AI can introduce new possibilities to multiple spheres of human lives, such as medicine, finance, transportation, and entertainment. It offers the possibility of bypassing repetitive work, decision making is becoming more accurate, and scientific research becomes more effective and, as a result, better solutions for complex issues are created.

Here are some examples of Artificial Intelligence (AI) applications across various domains:

Recommendation Systems: Online streaming platforms including Netflix, Max, SonyLIV, Spotify etc uses AI algorithms to analyse user preferences and behaviour patterns, then tailor suggestions of content, products, or music based on an individual's tastes.

Virtual Personal Assistants: Virtual personal assistants like Siri, Google Assistant and Amazon Alexa work through AI algorithms to get natural language query sense and carry out tasks and provide personalized responses.

Image Recognition: Image recognition systems powered by AI, which are used in facial recognition, medical imaging diagnostics, and self-driving cars, can detect objects, people or patterns in images with the utmost precision.

Natural Language Processing (NLP): NLP algorithms make machines capable of understanding, interpreting and generating the human language on their own. Applications include sentiment analysis, chatbots, language translation, and voice recognition among others.

Autonomous Vehicles: Artificial intelligence plays a crucial part in self driving vehicles and autonomous drones because of its algorithms' ability to perceive the environment, make decisions, and navigate on its own without the need to intervene the human factor, technologies such as computer vision and machine learning are used to achieve this.

Fraud Detection: AI technology allows banks to detect fraud by comparing transaction patterns to detect anomalies, thus making it possible to flag suspicious activities instantly.

Healthcare Diagnosis: AI-based systems assist health care professionals in diagnosing diseases, reading medical images, predicting patient outcomes, as well as recommending treatment options, increasing accuracy and efficiency in healthcare.

Robotics: Highly intelligent AI robots are used in various fields such as manufacturing, logistics, healthcare, etc for surgery, production, packaging warehouse automation etc with precision and speed.

Gaming: AI algorithms are utilized in the gaming industry to make non-player character (NPC)'s intelligent, create game content dynamically, adjust the game difficulty based on the player's style, and produce realistic game experience via interaction.

Strong AI

Strong AI, also known as artificial general intelligence, is a computer that has the ability to take on problems that it has not been trained to work on —like a human. Strong AI would exhibit consciousness, self-awareness, and the ability to understand, learn, and adapt to new situations independently. Strong AI is still theoretical and it doesn't exist as of now. This is the type of AI we see in science fiction movies.

Weak AI

Weak AI, also referred to as narrow AI or specialized AI, looks after a defined context reproducing human intelligence (such as driving a car or human speech translation or content curation on websites, etc.).

Weak AI can perform a particular task at an extremely high level of efficiency. While these machines may seem intelligent, these machines are built on far more limited resources than the most humble human intelligence. These systems surpass humans at highly specialized tasks while at the same time are restricted within their domain and cannot perform tasks beyond their scope.

Examples of Weak AI includes Siri, Alexa, Google Search, Conversational bots, Email spam filters, Netflix's recommendations etc.

Limitations of Weak AI

- Limited to the types of specific tasks it can perform.
- Vulnerability to bias and faulty algorithms.
- Inability to match human capabilities in intelligence or creativity.
- May require continuous review and enhancement.

In summary, strong AI aims to emulate human-like intelligence across a broad range of tasks, while weak AI focuses on solving specific problems within well-defined domains.

IV

Evolution of Artificial Intelligence

History is many a time as written.

Stories about robots and machines that work on their own were written around 2700 years ago, during the time of Homer. But even long before Greeks, about 5000 to 8000 years ago, Indian Epics like the Ramayana and Mahabharata also talked about robots and self-moving machines. As per the books of Hinduism, such machines were created by the engineer GOD Vishwakarma. Greek mythology also talks about them, saying gods like Hephaestus and the craftsman Daedalus made them.

Barbarika is described as a powerful warrior with extra ordinary power. He could use many advanced weapons at once and solve math problems at lightning speed. He didn't think like a human; instead, he had a kind of artificial intelligence. He acted without considering the consequences and irrespective of faces. He could detach his head from his body and still see everything happening during the Kurukshetra war.

Krishna's weapon, the Sudarshana Chakra, had the unique ability to return to him without any additional assistance. This feature can be seen as an example of machine learning.

Kumbhakarna, Ravana's younger brother was represented with gigantic appearance used to sleep for six months and awakened for consuming food (energy refilling). Kumbhakarna was not human like instead was having the features of a humanoid robot.

According to the Ramayana, Ravana kidnapped Sita using the "Pushpak Viman," an automated flying chariot. The epic describes this flying vehicle as far more advanced than modern airplanes.

The Rig Veda explains that "Asura" doesn't mean 'demon.' Instead, it signifies 'the one who is not sura,' or individuals endowed with magical or extraordinary abilities.

Self-navigating ships, robotic swans, Automated servants were also mentioned in many of these books. Machines were able to recognize the voice of their masters.

It is more or less impossible to connect the earlier era to the current days. However, it is very clear that the concept of Artificial Intelligence and Machine Learning were there in human minds for several centuries and it continued to evolve.

Internet searches show that Alan Turing, a learner from Britain, wrote a paper in the 1950s called "Computer Machinery and Intelligence." In this paper, he talked about how to make smart machines and how to test their intelligence. His idea of decision science, artificial intelligence and machines solving the real-world problems stayed in paper because back then, computers couldn't store information, they could only execute commands.

Between 1957 and 1974, the field of artificial intelligence (AI) experienced a period of significant growth. During this time, computers became capable of storing information and became faster, cheaper, and more widely available. This led to further advancements and evolution in the field of AI.

In 1966, Joseph Weizenbaum created Eliza, one of the most celebrated computer programs of its time. Eliza was able to hold conversations with humans, often convincing them that the software had emotions similar to those of a human.

From 1982 to 1990, the Japanese government made significant investments in expert systems and other AI-related projects as part of their Fifth Generation Computer Project (FGCP). These efforts aimed to revolutionize computer processing, implement logic programming, and enhance artificial intelligence capabilities.

In 1997, IBM's Deep Blue defeated the world chess champion, Gary Kasparov, making history as the first computer to beat a reigning world chess champion.

In 2002, AI made its way into households with the introduction of Roomba, a robotic vacuum cleaner, marking the first time AI technology was widely adopted for home use.

In 2006, AI gained significant traction in the business world as major companies and corporations began integrating AI technologies into their operations.

In 2011, IBM's Watson made headlines by winning Jeopardy, a quiz show, where it demonstrated its ability to solve complex questions and riddles. Watson's victory showcased its capability to understand natural language and rapidly solve challenging queries.

In 2012, Google introduced a feature called "Google Now" as part of its Android app, which offered predictive information to users based on their interests and activities.

In 2014, chatbot named "Eugene Goostman" won the "Turing test.". The Turing test is a measure of a machine's ability to exhibit intelligent behaviour equivalent to, or indistinguishable from, that of a human. It was proposed by Alan Turing in 1950 as a way to test a machine's ability to demonstrate human-like intelligence. In the test, a human evaluator interacts with both a human and a machine (often through text-based communication) without knowing which is which. If the evaluator cannot reliably distinguish the machine from the human based on their responses, the machine is said to have passed the Turing test.

In 2015, Amazon released the Amazon Echo, a smart speaker equipped with the voice-controlled virtual assistant Alexa.

In 2018, IBM, Airbus, and the German Aerospace Center DLR collaborated to develop CIMON, the first robot sent into space to assist astronauts.

In the year 2018, OpenAI released GPT (Generative Pre-trained Transformer), which paved the way for subsequent Large Language Models (LLMs).

In 2018, Google demonstrated an AI program called "Duplex," which acted as a virtual assistant. It successfully made a hairdresser appointment over the phone, and the person on the other end didn't realize they were speaking with a machine.

In 2020, during the COVID-19 pandemic, the University of Oxford developed an AI test called Curial to rapidly identify COVID-19 in emergency room patients.

In 2021, OpenAI introduced DALL-E, a multimodal AI system capable of generating images from textual prompts.

In 2022, the launch of ChatGPT marked a significant milestone in the advancement of AI technology. Within five days of its release, ChatGPT attracted over a million users, and within two months, it exceeded 100 million users, making it the fastest-growing consumer app at the time. However, this record was later surpassed by Facebook's Threads app. Threads, upon its launch, quickly gained momentum, with over 1 million users in just one hour. Remarkably, within two days, Threads reached an impressive 70 million users.

In 2023, the world of AI witnessed several significant developments.

OpenAI launched GPT-4, the latest iteration of its powerful language model, showcasing advancements in natural language processing. Google introduced AI-powered search capabilities, enhancing the efficiency and accuracy of search results. These milestones represent the ongoing evolution and integration of AI technologies into various aspects of our daily lives, from communication to information retrieval.

As of today, Artificial Intelligence is Everywhere

When you book a flight, an artificial intelligence, not a person, often decides how much you pay. At the airport, an AI system watches what you do. And when you're on the plane, a computer assists the pilot fly you to your destination.

AI systems are also starting to decide if you can get a loan, receive welfare, or get a job.

Some governments have bought weapons that can fight on their own, and they're using AI systems to spy on and control people.

AI systems help make the software you use and translate the words you read. Voice-controlled helpers, like Siri or Alexa, are in many homes now. And self-driving cars are becoming a reality.

AI powered Recommendation engines decide what you see on social media , what videos are suggested to you on YouTube and other OTT platforms, what products are shown to you online, and they're not just suggesting things anymore; they're also creating content like images and texts.

Artificial intelligence is here now, and it's changing our world in ways that used to only happen in science fiction movies. It is a technology that already impacts all of us.

Just two decades ago, the world was very different.

We haven't gotten any smarter about how we are coding artificial intelligence, so what changed?

It is the availability of Data and its storage.

V

Machine Learning

Machine learning is the science of developing algorithms and statistical models that enable computer systems to improve their performance on a specific task through learning from data, without being explicitly programmed.

The primary goal of machine learning is to develop models that can generalize patterns from the input data and make accurate predictions or decisions on new, unseen data.

In simple terms, machine learning is like teaching computers to learn from examples and experiences, rather than being explicitly programmed to do a specific task. It's a way to make computers smart and capable of improving their performance over time.

Imagine you want a computer to recognize pictures of cats. Instead of telling the computer exactly what a cat looks like, you show it lots of pictures of cats and say, "These are cats." The computer learns from these examples and figures out on its own what features make up a cat. Now, when you show it a new picture, it can recognize whether it's a cat or not based on what it learned.

In essence, machine learning is about training computers to learn patterns from data so they can make predictions or decisions without being explicitly programmed for every detail. It's like teaching a computer to think and make sense of information by itself.

The process of machine learning typically involves the following steps:

1. Data Collection: Gathering relevant data that the machine learning model will use to learn patterns and make predictions.

2. Data Pre-processing: Cleaning, organizing, and transforming the raw data to make it suitable for training a machine learning model.

3. Feature Extraction: Identifying and selecting relevant features (variables) from the data that will be used by the model to make predictions.

4. Model Training: Using an algorithm, the machine learning model is trained on a labelled dataset, where the input data is paired with corresponding output labels. The model learns to map inputs to outputs by adjusting its parameters based on patterns in the data.

5. Model Evaluation: Assessing the performance of the trained model using separate datasets not seen during training. This helps determine how well the model generalizes to new, unseen data.

6. Model Deployment: If the model performs well, it can be deployed to make predictions or decisions on new data in real-world applications.

What is a pattern?

In mathematics, a pattern refers to a recurring arrangement of numbers, shapes, colors, or anything iterative. These patterns can be associated with any type of event or object. When a set of numbers follows a specific rule or sequence, it is considered as a pattern. Patterns are sometimes referred to as sequences and can be finite or infinite in length.

For example, look at the series 2, 4, 6, 8, and ....? Further ?

Each number in this sequence increases by 2. Hence, the following number in the series would be adding 8 and 2, so the answer would be 10.

Few examples of numerical patterns are:
10, 20, 30, 40, 50, 60, 70, 80, 90.....
Even numbers pattern -: 2, 4, 6, 8, 10, 12, 14, 16, 18, ...
Odd numbers pattern -: 3, 5, 7, 9, 11, 13, 15, 17, 19, ...
Fibonacci numbers pattern -: 1, 1, 2, 3, 5, 8 ,13, 21, ... and so on.
In the context of AI, a pattern refers to a regular, recognizable, and recurring structure or sequence observed within data. Patterns are being developed in various forms, such as relationships, trends, or correlations, and they are typically identified through data analysis techniques like machine learning algorithms or statistical methods.

For example, in image recognition, patterns represent unique features about objects or objects themselves which in turn enables AI to sort and identify objects just by using those patterns.
In natural language processing, patterns may include recurring sequences of words or phrases that convey specific meanings or sentiments, and therefore use it to check the sentiment analysis or language translation.
Identifying and understanding patterns within data is essential for AI systems to learn from past experiences, make predictions, and take informed decisions in various applications, ranging from predictive analytics and recommendation systems to robotics and self-driving vehicles.

Patterns can appear in various forms, such as

Visual Patterns: In pattern recognition for image tasks, patterns may involve shapes, textures, colours or the relationship between pixels at specific places which help to generate different objects or different scenes on the basis of characters they pick from the pixels.

Temporal Patterns: In the time-series case, specifics would be found/ developed over time featuring such things, as the trends, cycles, or seasonal variations.

Sequential Patterns: In sequential Data such as text or speech, patterns can be featured as word sequences which may describe provision of meaning and context.

Statistical Patterns: The study of numerical data sometimes entails statistical relationships between variables, such as correlations, distributions, or outliers.

AI algorithms including machine learning and deep learning models which are trained to identify and seek out patterns from data. These patterns, once discovered, become a tool which can be utilized for many tasks including classification, prediction, anomaly detection, and decision-making, among many others. This is the vital ability that is essential to make AI systems successful in any area of application and among any number of domains.

What are the types of Machine learning?

Machine Learning can be broadly categorized into three main types, based on the learning styles and approaches:

Supervised Learning: The model is trained on a labelled dataset, where each input is associated with a corresponding output label.

Examples:

- Classification: Identifying whether an email is spam or not.
- Regression: Predicting house prices based on features like size, location, etc.

Unsupervised Learning: Unsupervised learning deals with unlabelled data, and the algorithm is tasked with finding patterns, relationships, or structures within the data without explicit guidance.

Examples:

- Customer Segmentation: Grouping customers based on their purchasing behaviour without prior knowledge of customer segments. This can help businesses tailor marketing strategies for each group.
- Fraud Detection / Anomaly Detection: Detecting unusual patterns or outliers in financial transactions that may indicate

fraudulent activity. This is particularly useful in credit card fraud detection.

Reinforcement Learning: The model learns by interacting with an environment, receiving feedback in the form of rewards or penalties.

Examples:

- Self-Driving Cars: Reinforcement learning can be used to train autonomous vehicles to make driving decisions based on environmental feedback, traffic conditions, and safety considerations.

- Personalized Content Recommendations: Recommending content to users based on their interactions and preferences. The system learns from user feedback (watched movies, clicked links) to improve recommendations.

Machine learning is applied across a wide range of domains, including image and speech recognition, natural language processing, recommendation systems, autonomous vehicles, healthcare, finance, and more. The specific algorithm or technique chosen depends on the nature of the task and the characteristics of the available data.

Learning Type	Focus	Learning Method	Examples
Supervised Learning	Prediction	Classification: Predicting a category (e.g., spam or not spam email) Regression: Predicting a continuous value (e.g., housing price)	Image classification (cat vs dog) Sentiment analysis (positive, negative, or neutral review) Spam filtering
Unsupervised Learning	Identifying patterns and relationships	Clustering: Grouping data points based on similarities (e.g., customer segmentation) Dimensionality Reduction: Reducing the number of features in a dataset (e.g., image compression)	Market segmentation (clustering customers based on buying habits) Recommender systems (suggesting similar products) Anomaly detection (identifying unusual patterns in data)
Reinforcement Learning	Control and optimization	Learning by receiving feedback (rewards or penalties) for actions in a simulated environment	Training game playing AI, Robot control

Types of ML

How is Machine learning related to AI?

The term AI and ML may seem to be used interchangeably, especially when referring to the use of big data, predictive analytics, digital transformations and other similar topics. To some extent it is clear that artificial intelligence (AI) and machine learning (ML) are closely connected fields. On the other hand, these two technologies differ in many areas including scope, applications, and more.

AI and ML are the key component of technology that is getting used by businesses to manage large data, assisted decision-making , create real-time recommendations and insights, in addition to accurate forecasts and predictions.

So what is the difference between ML and AI ? How these two are connected? What do these mean for organizations in reality?

Even though AI and ML are not exactly same, there exists a very strong connection between the two. The simplest way to understand how AI and ML relate to each other is,

Artificial intelligence	Machine learning
AI stand for a broader concept of allowing a machine or system to think, understand, act, or learn like a human.	ML can be simply defined as the use of AI by machines in which they can extract existing knowledge from the data and learn from themselves without the intervention of human experts.
Aims to create intelligent agents that can mimic human-like cognitive functions, such as reasoning, problem-solving, understanding natural language, and learning from experience.	Specifically concerned about developing algorithms that allow machines to learn patterns and insights from data, adapting and improving their performance over time.
Encompasses various approaches, including rule-based systems, symbolic reasoning, and expert systems. Not all AI systems rely on learning from data.	Primarily revolves around learning from data. ML algorithms learn patterns and relationships within the data to make predictions or decisions without explicit programming.
Quite a broad field of applications.	The choice of applications is limited.
AI-systems use logic and reasoning trees to learn, reason, and self-amend.	ML systems rely on statistical methods and the machine can self-correct when the new data is presented to it.
May or may not involve learning from data. It can rely on pre-defined rules and logic	Involves a continuous learning process. ML models learn from data, receive feedback, and adjust their predictions or decisions based on new information.

AI vs ML

VI

Large Language Model

Large Language Model is a type of artificial intelligence (AI) model trained on massive amounts of text data to understand and generate human-like language. LLMs are incredibly complex and powerful, capable of performing a wide range of tasks such as:

- **Content Creation:** Imagine having a tireless writer churning out marketing copy, product descriptions, or even scripts. LLMs can assist with various content creation tasks, freeing up human creativity for more strategic endeavours. From poems to scripts to marketing copy, LLMs can adapt to various styles and formats.

- **Personalized Learning:** Education can become more engaging and individualized with LLMs. These models can answer student questions in a personalized way, provide feedback on writing, and even tailor learning experiences to individual needs.
- **Customer Service:** Chatbots powered by LLMs can offer 24/7 support, answer customer queries accurately, and even handle complex conversations, enhancing customer experience and reducing wait times.

- **Language Barriers:** LLMs are poised to become powerful tools for machine translation, breaking down language barriers and facilitating communication across cultures. Imagine seamlessly translating documents, conducting multilingual conversations, or accessing information in foreign languages with ease.
- **Research:** LLMs can analyse massive amounts of text data, uncovering hidden patterns, trends, and insights that would be impossible for humans alone. This can accelerate research in various fields, from social sciences to medicine and beyond.
- **Summarizing text:** LLMs can condense large amounts of text into concise summaries, highlighting key points and information.

How are LLMs Trained?

LLMs are trained using a technique called deep learning. This involves feeding the model with massive amounts of text data, such as books, articles, code, and websites. The model then analyses this data and learns to identify patterns and relationships between words. Over time, the model becomes increasingly adept at understanding and generating human-like language.

Several critical factors contribute to an LLM's strengths:

- **Data Size:** The amount of training data plays a pivotal role. The more text the model ingests, the more nuanced and versatile its understanding of language becomes. Think of it as the foundation upon which its abilities are built.
- **Model Architecture:** The specific structure of the neural network, the underlying technology powering the LLM, influences its capabilities. Just like different tools are suited for different tasks, the architecture determines the model's strengths and weaknesses.
- **Training Objectives:** What do you want your LLM to be good at? Setting specific objectives during training guides the model's

development. Do you want it to excel at generating creative text formats, accurately translating languages, or answering questions informatively? Each objective shapes its unique skillset.

Examples of LLMs

- **GPT-3 (OpenAI):** This highly influential model excels in generating different creative text formats, translating languages, and answering your questions in an informative way. It has been used for various tasks, including generating marketing copy, writing poetry, and translating books.
- **Megatron-Turing NLG (NVIDIA):** This model excels at generating coherent and engaging text, particularly for narrative formats. It has been used to create realistic dialogue for virtual assistants and chatbots.
- **Gemini (Google AI):** This model can generate different creative text formats, translate languages, write different kinds of creative content, and answer your questions in an informative way, constantly learning and adapting to your needs and preferences. Gemini is focusing on multimodal understanding and generation.
- **Jurassic-1 Jumbo (AI21 Labs):** This model focuses on factual language understanding and question answering, making it suitable for tasks like generating reports and summarizing information.
- **BLOOM (Allen Institute for Artificial Intelligence):** This model focuses on factual language understanding and reasoning, making it suitable for tasks like generating summaries and answering open-ended questions.
- **WuDao 2.0 (BAAI):** This Chinese LLM excels at understanding and generating text in Chinese, with applications in areas like education, healthcare, and customer service.

What is AI Glass ?

AI Glass is a comprehensive end-to-end solution by Tata Elxsi for managing the lifecycle of AI models, encompassing both machine learning and deep learning models. It incorporates advanced algorithms to monitor data drift and model drift, common occurrences in environments deploying numerous AI models in production settings.

VII

LangChain

Simplifying LLM Application Development

LangChain is a framework designed to simplify the development of applications powered by large language models (LLMs). It provides a modular approach that breaks down complex tasks into smaller, reusable components called "chains." These chains can perform various functions, including data retrieval, language modeling, and reasoning, enabling the development of sophisticated applications without needing to build everything from scratch.

Key Features of LangChain:

- **Modular Design:** Chains can be combined and customized to create complex workflows tailored to specific needs.
- **Flexibility:** Supports various LLMs and can be extended with custom components, offering adaptability to different project requirements.
- **Context-Awareness:** Allows chains to access and utilize context information (e.g., prompts, previous outputs) to generate more relevant and consistent results.
- **Reasoning Capabilities:** Enables applications to make decisions and take actions based on the processed information, going beyond simple text generation.

Potential Applications:

- **Chatbots:** Build conversational bots with enhanced understanding and response capabilities.
- **Document Analysis and Summarization:** Extract key information and generate summaries from text documents.
- **Code Analysis and Generation:** Assist with code understanding, debugging, and potentially even code generation.
- **Creative Text Formats:** Generate different creative text formats like poems, scripts, etc., tailored to specific requirements.
- **Custom Text-to-Speech:** Create voice applications with specific accents or regional languages tailored to your needs.

Benefits of Using LangChain:

- **Reduced Development Time:** Simplifies LLM integration, accelerating application development compared to building from scratch.
- **Increased Efficiency:** Modular architecture promotes code reusability and efficient use of LLM capabilities.
- **Enhanced Functionality:** Context-awareness and reasoning features enable applications with more sophisticated capabilities.
- **Improved Maintainability:** Modular design facilitates easier maintenance and updates to applications.

Considerations:

- **Learning Curve:** Understanding LangChain and building effective chains requires some learning and technical expertise.

- **Maturity:** While promising, LangChain is a relatively new framework, and its long-term stability and ecosystem need further observation. As of the beginning of 2024, LangChain primarily focuses on integrating with Bard and Jurassic-1 Jumbo LLMs.

- LangChain offers a promising approach to building LLM-powered applications. By understanding its features, functionalities, and considerations, you can assess its potential to simplify and empower your development efforts. LangChain is an open-source project and can access its code and documentation freely. Also several online resources and community forums are available to help you learn more about LangChain and get started with building your own applications.

VIII
Deep Learning

Deep learning is a type of machine learning that includes neural networks with multiple hidden layers through which the data is processed, allowing the machine to go "deep" in its learning. Deep learning models are capable of learning directly from raw data to produce the desired output, without the need for intermediate processing or feature extraction steps. These networks imitate the human brain networks and can be used for tasks such as image recognition, speech understanding, and language processing.

Deep learning works by using artificial neural networks to learn from data. Neural networks are made up of layers of interconnected nodes, and each node is responsible for learning a specific feature of the data. In the case of an image recognition network, the first layer of nodes can detect edges, the second layer nodes can identify shapes and the next layer of nodes can see objects.

As the network learns, the weights on the connections between the nodes are adjusted so that the network can better classify the data. During the training procedure various methods are applied like supervised learning, unsupervised learning, and reinforcement learning.

Neural networks, once they are trained, can be used for making predictions with new data that they receive.

Deep Learning Vs Machine Learning

While both deep learning and machine learning aim to teach computers to perform tasks without explicit programming, they differ in their approach and application. Deep learning focuses on neural network architectures with multiple layers (deep architectures) and excels at handling unstructured data, while machine learning encompasses a broader set of techniques and requires manual feature engineering in many cases.

Facebook uses deep learning algorithms to automatically tag people in photos , Google Photos uses it to organize and categorize images.

Deep learning applications

Deep learning can be used in a wide variety of applications across domains including:

- **Image recognition:** Utilized for identifying objects and features within images, including people, animals, and places.
- **Natural language processing:** To help understand the meaning of text, such as customer support, sentiment analysis, email filtering etc.
- **Speech Recognition:** Deep learning techniques are utilized in speech recognition systems, enabling accurate transcription and voice command recognition. Virtual assistants like Siri and Google Assistant leverage deep learning for speech understanding.
- **Medical Diagnosis and Healthcare:** Deep learning is applied in medical imaging for tasks like tumor detection, pathology, and radiology. It is also used for predicting disease outcomes and drug discovery.
- **Finance:** In finance, deep learning models analyze large datasets to make predictions about market trends, stock prices, and

financial risks. Algorithmic trading and fraud detection benefit from deep learning applications.

- **Cybersecurity**: Deep learning enhances cybersecurity by detecting and preventing cyber threats. It can analyze patterns of network traffic to identify abnormal behavior indicative of potential security breaches.

IX

Generative AI

What is GEN AI ?

Generative Artificial Intelligence refers to a category of artificial intelligence, that are designed to generate new original content, that is not explicitly present in the training data. Unlike traditional AI systems that are rule-based or follow predefined patterns, generative AI has the ability to create novel outputs, whether it be images, text, music, or other types of content, by learning patterns and structures from existing data.

Gen AI is like a creative tool that can make pictures, write texts, compose music, and more. It's good at making things that look real and different, which is handy for art, design, and entertainment. However, it also highlights ethical considerations, as it can potentially be used to generate misleading or malicious content.

Key aspects of Gen AI include:

1. Data Generation:

Gen AI is particularly known for its ability to create new, realistic data instances. This can be applied to various domains, such as generating images, videos, text, music, and more. For example, in image generation, it can create realistic faces of people who don't exist. In text generation, it can generate coherent paragraphs of text based on a given prompt.

2. Variety and Novelty:

Generative models aim to capture the underlying patterns and structures of the training data, enabling them to produce diverse and novel outputs that share characteristics with the original data.

3. Challenges:

Training generative models can be challenging, and ensuring that the generated content is both diverse and high-quality requires careful tuning. Ethical considerations also come into play, as generative AI can potentially be misused to create deep fakes or misleading content.

Generative Adversarial Networks (GANs)

Imagine two artists locked in a creative competition: one making new paintings, the other judging their authenticity. This is essentially the core idea behind Generative Adversarial Networks (GANs), a powerful AI technique for creating realistic, never-before-seen data.

The Creative Genius: The **generator** network starts creating paintings or stories. These creations are so good, they might trick someone into thinking they were made by a real person!

The Critic: The **discriminator** network acts as the art critic, carefully examining each piece and trying to separate genuine masterpieces from the generator's forgeries.

The Adversarial Dance: As they compete, both networks improve. The generator, fuelled by the critic's feedback, refines its skills, producing progressively more convincing creations.

The critic, constantly challenged, sharpens its ability to sniff out fakes.

The Grand Prize: After countless rounds, the ultimate goal is for the generator to become so skilled that its creations are indistinguishable from real data.

Where GANs excel: This innovative approach unveils thrilling opportunities, Creating realistic portraits of individuals who don't exist. Crafting original musical compositions or artistic genres. Pioneering ground breaking medications or materials via simulated modelling.

To define GAN

GANs are a class of artificial intelligence algorithms used in unsupervised machine learning. It consist of two neural networks, the generator and the discriminator, which are trained simultaneously through a competitive process.

The generator network creates new data instances that resemble the training data, while the discriminator network acts as a classifier that learns to distinguish between real data instances and fake data generated by the generator. During training, the generator and discriminator are trained in an adversarial manner, with the generator trying to produce increasingly realistic samples to fool the discriminator, while the discriminator learns to become better at distinguishing between real and fake samples.

The ultimate goal of GANs is to produce high-quality synthetic data that is indistinguishable from real data. GANs have applications in various domains, including image generation, data augmentation, text-to-image synthesis, and video generation. While powerful, GANs aren't perfect. Training them can be tricky, requiring careful balancing and monitoring. Also, ethical considerations are crucial, as they can be misused to create deceptive content.

X

Natural Language Processing

A branch of Artificial Intelligence dedicated to bridging the gap between computers and our intricate world of words. NLP aims to equip machines with the ability to not just process text, but truly understand its meaning and nuances, just like we do.

Think of it like teaching a computer a new language – a language teeming with idioms, sarcasm, and ever-evolving slang. NLP solves this challenge through two key pillars:

1. Natural Language Understanding (NLU): Imagine a computer that grasps the nuances of human speech. NLU makes this possible by tackling tasks like:

- **Linguistic analysis:** Understanding the grammatical structure of sentences, identifying parts of speech like verbs, nouns, and adjectives.
- **Entity recognition:** Spotlighting key entities within text, like people, places, and organizations, crucial for understanding context.
- **Semantic parsing:** Uncovering the deeper meaning of sentences, analysing relationships between words and concepts.

- **Sentiment analysis:** Identifying the emotional tone of text, determining whether it is positive, negative, or neutral.

2. Natural Language Generation (NLG): Have you ever interacted with a chatbot that feels surprisingly human-like? NLG makes this magic happen, enabling computers to produce language that mimics human communication styles. This includes tasks like:

- **Text summarization:** Simplifies lengthy texts into concise summaries, extracting key points for efficient information processing.
- **Dialogue systems:** Creating chatbots that can hold conversations, answer questions, and engage with users in a natural way.
- **Machine translation:** Breaking down language barriers, enabling seamless communication and information exchange across diverse cultures.
- **Creative text formats:** Pushing the boundaries of language, NLG can even generate poems, scripts, musical pieces, and other creative text formats.

The Impact of NLP

NLP has seamlessly integrated into our everyday routines, extending far beyond academic purposes, Here are some use cases,

- **Revolutionizing communication:** Machine translation tools powered by NLP bridge language barriers, fostering global understanding and collaboration.
- **Search Engines:** NLP algorithms power the magic behind search engines like Google and Bing, understanding your queries and delivering relevant results with incredible accuracy.
- **Personalized experiences:** From suggesting relevant products to recommending news articles, NLP algorithms tailor content and services to individual preferences.

- **Unlocking information:** NLP helps us navigate the vast ocean of online text, enabling efficient search engines and insightful data analysis.
- **Social Media Analysis:** NLP tools help analyze vast amounts of social media data, understanding public sentiment, tracking trends, and providing valuable insights for businesses and organizations.
- **Empowering healthcare:** NLP assists with medical diagnosis by analyzing patient records and generating reports, potentially aiding earlier interventions and improved outcomes.
- **Virtual Reality and Augmented Reality Experiences:** NLP helps create interactive and immersive experiences in VR/AR by enabling natural language interaction with virtual environments.

The Future of NLP: As technology continues to evolve, the potential of NLP expands exponentially. Imagine AI assistants that understand complex instructions and respond with empathy, or educational tools that personalize learning based on individual needs. These are just glimpses into the future where NLP will play a central role in shaping our interactions with the digital world.

As of the beginning of 2024, here are some examples of GEN AI applications that can help you save time in accomplishing your daily goals.

Please note that pricing and features may vary over time, so it's always a good idea to check the latest information on the provider's website.

Text Generators: Generative AI for creating articles, conversations, Emails, blog posts etc

- **ChatGPT** : Designed for conversational contexts, to generate human-like responses in chat-based applications, Cannot provide real-time information
- **Gemini** : Focuses on factual language and creative text formats - Claims to be more reliable and informative than competitors ,

Still learning.

- **Copy.ai:** Focuses on marketing and advertising copywriting, offering templates and AI assistance for various content types.
- **Jasper:** Tailored for marketing and sales content creation, including website copy, ad copy, and blog posts. Generates various content formats (blog posts, ads, scripts) - Long-form content capabilities - Brand voice customization - Integrates with other tools.
- **Writesonic:** Provides AI-powered assistance for crafting product descriptions, social media posts, and other marketing materials.
- **Sudowrite:** Designed for fiction writing, offering prompts, character development tools, and scene generation to aid writers.
- **Headline Studio by CoSchedule :** Generates catchy headlines and titles for different content formats.
- **Articoolo:** Provides automated article writing and rewriting services, focusing on SEO and content marketing.
- **Stealth Writer:** Specifically designed for content marketing and SEO, Creates human likes content, good for rewriting, Has built in plagiarism Check.
- **Anyword:** Specifically designed for marketing and advertising professionals, this AI tool offers unique features like A/B testing, data-driven copywriting, and personalized content generation across various channels (e.g., emails, social media ads, product descriptions.

Presentation Creators: Generative AI converts text to presentations.

- **Simplified.com:** Uses AI to convert text outlines into visually-appealing presentations with layouts, images, and text suggestions.
- **Slides AI:** Creates presentations from text outlines, offering different design styles and customization options.

- **Beautiful.ai:** Employs AI to design professional and visually stunning presentations with minimal effort.
- **Designs.ai:** Uses AI to create presentations with unique layouts, themes, and animations, ideal for data-driven presentations.
- **Tome:** Generates presentations from text and images, focusing on aesthetic design and storytelling.
- **DeckRobot:** Creates AI-powered presentations from text outlines, offering customization options and collaboration features.
- **StoryAI:** Helps craft compelling narratives for your presentations with AI-powered storyboarding and scripting assistance.
- **Canva :** Converts your Canva documents into presentation slides with AI, maintaining the design and content.
- **Kroma.ai:** This tool uses AI to personalize presentations for individual viewers based on their interests and demographics. It's useful for targeted presentations.

Image Generators: These tools can turn text into images.

- **DALL-E 2 (OpenAI):** This highly advanced tool creates incredibly realistic and creative images based on your text prompts. However, it currently requires paid access and has limited availability.
- **Midjourney:** Generates high-quality, artistic images with diverse styles and themes. It operates through a Discord server and offers subscription plans.
- **Limewire AI:** Generates 3D objects and environments based on textual descriptions, useful for creative projects or product design concepts. It offers paid plans.
- **Runway ML:** Provides a platform for exploring and using various AI models, including some for image generation and editing, offering flexibility and customization for experienced users. It has free and paid options.

- **DreamStudio (Stable Diffusion):** Provides access to various diffusion models, including Stable Diffusion, allowing for more control over image generation and customization. It operates through browser access and offers paid plans.
- **NightCafe Creator:** Offers access to several AI algorithms like DALL-E 2, Stable Diffusion, and others, allowing for experimentation with different styles and results. It has both free and paid options.
- **Craiyon** : A free and accessible option that generates creative images based on your text prompts, though with limitations in detail and realism compared to paid tools.
- **Starry AI:** Generates vibrant and artistic images based on your text prompts, offering various styles and customization options. It operates through a browser with paid plans.
- **Artbreeder:** Leverages AI to explore and create unique images through breeding and manipulating existing ones, focusing on artistic exploration and experimentation. It has free and paid options.

Video Generators: Generative AI for text-to-video conversion.

- **Synthesia:** Creates highly realistic AI-powered videos with human actors delivering your text script, ideal for marketing, e-learning, and presentations.
- **Pictory:** Converts text and images into engaging social media video formats, offering easy-to-use templates and customization options. Allows adding images, videos, and music to text-based videos.
- **InVideo:** Provides a comprehensive platform for video creation, including AI-powered features like text-to-video, animation, and editing tools.
- **Lumen5:** Generates video presentations from your text and images, focusing on educational and explainer-type content.
- **DeepBrain AI:** Offers a variety of AI-powered video creation tools, including text-to-video, animation, and voiceover

generation.

- **Runway ML:** Offers access to various AI models for video editing and generation, including text-to-video capabilities, requiring more technical expertise.
- **Descript:** Primarily an editing tool, Descript uses AI to transcribe audio, edit captions, and even change the speaker's voice, adding AI capabilities to your video editing workflow.
- **Wondershare Filmora:** Provides video editing tools with some AI-powered features like automatic scene detection, object removal, and style transfer.

Audio Voice Generators: Generative AI converts text to sound for audiobooks, voiceovers, and advertisements.

- **Narakeet:** Offers numerous Indian English and Indian regional language voices like Hindi, Bengali, and Tamil. Customize pitch, speed, and emotion for engaging content.
- **Murf:** Offers a variety of high-quality voices in different languages and accents, allowing for customization of pitch, speed, and emotion. It's suitable for creating voiceovers, explainer videos, and presentations. Provides some Indian English voices and allows custom accents for text-to-speech generation.
- **Play.ht:** Provides access to numerous AI voices with realistic and expressive qualities. It offers customizable speech styles and easy integration with video editing software. Offers Indian English voices and Hindi voices with expressive qualities.
- **NaturalReader:** Primarily focused on text-to-speech for reading purposes, but also allows creating voiceovers with various voices and customization options.
- **Descript:** Integrates text-to-speech functionality with audio editing tools, allowing you to create voiceovers and modify existing audio. It also offers voice cloning capabilities.
- **Lovo.ai:** Specializes in generating natural-sounding voices for audiobooks, e-learning modules, and other narration needs. It

offers multilingual support and a range of voices.

- **Speechify:** Combines text-to-speech with features like speed control, background music, and audio editing, suitable for creating audiobooks and podcasts.
- **Amazon Polly:** A highly popular cloud-based service offering multiple realistic voices in various languages with flexible customization options, suitable for diverse applications.
- **Google Text-to-Speech:** Google's own text-to-speech API offers a variety of high-quality voices with language support and customization options, suitable for web and mobile applications.
- **IBM Watson Text to Speech:** This service provides natural-sounding voices with customizable parameters and supports multiple languages, suitable for enterprise applications.
- **Resemble.ai:** Focuses on voice cloning, allowing you to create a synthetic voice that closely resembles a specific person's voice. It requires training data of the target voice.
- **Synthesia:** Combines text-to-speech with video creation, allowing you to generate videos with AI-powered narrators. It offers various voices and animation styles.
- **WellSaid Labs:** Provides custom-built AI voices tailored to specific brand identities or project requirements.
- **ElevenLabs:** Offers unique text-to-speech voices with deepfake capabilities, but has stricter usage guidelines and limitations.

XI
The Changing Landscape

Artificial intelligence will eliminate millions of current jobs and create millions of new ones. While AI advancements are automating many tasks and transforming various industries, it's not a simple replacement story.

The future workplace is being rewritten by artificial intelligence, and while some fear a series of job displacement, the reality is a more complex transformation and creation. While AI's automation capabilities are undeniable, its impact on the job market is a complex with multiple movements, each playing a distinct role

Jobs at Risk

- **From Filing Cabinets to Algorithms**: AI technologies can streamline and automate repetitive, routine tasks across various industries, such as manufacturing, customer service, and data entry. Imagine legal documents automatically categorized, medical records analysed with lightning speed, and financial transactions verified in milliseconds . Human employment will be uncertain for these positions.

- **The Factory Floor's:** The assembly line, once a place of human labor, is increasingly occupied by robots, their precise movements replacing the repetitive tasks once performed by human hands. From welding robots in car factories to automated assembly lines for electronics, AI is transforming the manufacturing landscape.
- **Behind the Wheel** : Autonomous delivery drones and self-driving trucks are already a reality and this will bring a potential shift in the transportation industry. While the future of taxi drivers and truck drivers remains uncertain, the need for skilled technicians, engineers, and infrastructure specialists to maintain and develop these systems is undeniable.

Jobs Less Likely to be Replaced

- **The Artist's Brush** : AI can generate creative outputs, but the spark of human imagination, the ability to evoke emotions and tell stories through art, music, and literature, remains uniquely human. The future of creative fields lies in the harmonious interplay of human and machine, with AI providing tools and inspiration, but artists retaining the power to move and inspire.
- **Humanizing Healthcare:** While AI can assist with medical diagnosis and treatment, the irreplaceable human touch of a doctor, their years of experience, and their ability to provide empathy and emotional support remain irreplaceable. The future of healthcare lies in collaboration, with AI augmenting human judgment, not replacing it.

- **From Text to Law, But Not Justice:** AI can analyze legal precedents and draft documents, but the complex world of law demands more than just data crunching. The courtroom symphony requires human lawyers, their ability to advocate, strategize, and navigate the nuances of human emotions and relationships.

Jobs Created by AI

- The rise of AI necessitates a new breed of conductor – the AI developer. These skilled professionals design, build, and maintain the complex systems that power the AI revolution, ensuring they function efficiently and ethically.
- Prompt engineering specialists play a crucial role in shaping the behavior of AI systems by designing and refining prompts or instructions given to AI models. They ensure that prompts effectively generate the desired responses and align with organizational goals and ethical considerations.
- Making sense of the vast data generated by AI systems requires the expertise of a data scientist. These individuals collect, analyse, and interpret this data, extracting insights that fuel innovation and inform decision-making across industries.
- Cybersecurity specialists become the guardians of this digital ecosystem, protecting systems from cyberattacks and ensuring the security of sensitive data.

Overall Impact:

- **Job displacement:** Some jobs will undoubtedly be lost due to automation, leading to unemployment and economic disruption.
- **Job creation:** AI will also create new jobs in fields like AI development, data analysis, and cybersecurity.
- **Job transformation:** Many existing jobs will evolve, requiring new skills and knowledge to work alongside AI effectively.

Preparing for the future:

- **Focus on lifelong learning:** Investing in continuous education and acquiring new skills will be crucial for navigating the changing job market.

- **Develop human-specific skills:** Cultivating critical thinking, creativity, and emotional intelligence will give humans an edge over AI in many fields.
- **Embrace adaptation:** Staying flexible and open to new opportunities will be key to thriving in the AI-powered world.

The future of employment belongs to those who can adapt and evolve. Continuous learning, a commitment to acquiring new skills, and the ability to embrace change will be the key to navigating the ever-shifting job market landscape. Whether it's learning to work alongside AI, developing expertise in new technologies, or cultivating human-centric skills like critical thinking and creativity, the individuals who can adapt to the rhythm of change will be the ones who thrive in the AI-powered future.

XII

Impact of AI on project managers

Artificial intelligence (AI) is undoubtedly causing a stir in the project management world, offering both challenges and opportunities for project managers. Here's a breakdown of its potential impact:

Positive Impacts:

- **Efficiency and Productivity:** AI automates repetitive tasks like scheduling, resource allocation, and progress tracking, freeing up time for project managers to focus on higher-level strategic thinking and decision-making.
- **Data-driven insights:** AI analyses vast amounts of project data to identify risks, predict outcomes, and suggest improvement strategies. This empowers project managers to make informed decisions based on objective data rather than intuition alone.
- **Improved communication and collaboration:** AI-powered tools can facilitate communication and collaboration within teams, translating languages, generating reports, and providing real-time updates.

- **Risk Mitigation:** AI proactively identifies potential risks based on historical data and patterns, allowing project managers to take preventive measures and minimize disruptions.
- **Personalized Management:** AI can tailor its support to individual project managers, suggesting best practices and learning preferences, optimizing their individual workflows.

Negative Impacts:

- **Job displacement:** Some project management tasks might be completely automated, potentially leading to job displacement for some individuals.
- **Overreliance on AI:** Dependence on AI for decision-making could hinder critical thinking and problem-solving skills, essential for managing unforeseen challenges.
- **Ethical considerations:** Bias inherent in AI algorithms could lead to unfair outcomes in project planning and resource allocation. Ensuring ethical and transparent use of AI is crucial.
- **Skill gap:** Transitioning to AI-powered project management might require acquiring new skills in data analysis, technology integration, and AI oversight.
- **Resistance to change:** Adapting to new technologies and workflows can be challenging for some individuals, requiring effective change management strategies.

Overall Impact:

AI is not meant to replace project managers, but rather to augment their capabilities and effectiveness. The future of project management likely involves a **partnership between humans and AI**, where humans bring their judgment, experience, emotions and leadership skills, while AI assists with data-driven decision-making, automation, and optimization.

Here are some tips for project managers to thrive in the AI era:

- **Embrace lifelong learning:** Continuously acquire new skills in data analysis, AI literacy, and technology integration.
- **Focus on human-specific skills:** Sharpen your leadership, communication, and critical thinking skills, areas where AI currently falls short.
- **Become an AI champion:** Advocate for responsible and ethical use of AI within your organization, ensuring transparency and fairness.
- **Partner with AI, not be replaced by it:** View AI as a powerful tool to enhance your skills and decision-making, not a threat to your job.

The impact of AI on project management is still unfolding, but by understanding its potential and proactively adapting, project managers can play a vital role in shaping a future where humans and AI collaborate to achieve even greater success.

Some of the tools which project / program managers can explore

- **ClickUp.com** offers a robust AI-powered workload management feature that analyses team capacity and suggests task assignments to avoid overallocation. It can also configure automated email responses for task assignments, updates, and deadlines.
- **Notion.so** utilizes AI to streamline the planning phase by generating automated task suggestions based on completed tasks and project templates. Notion integrates with email services like Gmail to trigger automated email notifications based on task completions or project updates.
- **Wrike.com** leverages AI for intelligent scheduling, suggesting deadlines and dependencies based on historical data and resource availability. It can be configured to send automated email notifications to team members when deadlines shift or task dependencies change.
- **Beforesunset.ai** This AI-powered tool focuses on resource optimization, using machine learning to analyze team skills and

project requirements for optimal team allocation.

- **HiveMind (hive.com)** This project management platform uses machine learning to identify potential risks and roadblocks early in the project lifecycle. It analyzes data to predict project outcomes and suggest corrective actions. HiveMind can be set up to send automated email alerts when potential roadblocks are detected.
- **Forecast.app** - Utilizes AI to automate task assignments, optimize resource allocation, and provide predictive analytics for project planning and management. It also offers automatic email notifications to keep project managers informed.
- **Scoro.com** incorporates AI to assist with scheduling, resource allocation, and project progress tracking, enabling teams to make data-driven decisions.
- **Teamwork Desk (teamwork.com)** offers AI-powered chatbots for collaboration, but it also integrates with email to trigger automated responses based on project updates or task completions.
- **LiquidPlanner.com** employs AI algorithms for dynamic scheduling, priority-based task management, and real-time project tracking, improving project outcomes.
- **Proggio.com** integrates AI to analyze project data, identify patterns, and provide insights for better decision-making and resource allocation.
- **Planview.com** leverages AI for strategic portfolio management, project prioritization, and resource optimization, enabling organizations to align projects with business goals.
- **Zoho Projects** - This Indian homegrown platform offers AI-powered features like workload management, real-time analytics, and smart search.
- **ProofHub.com** This project management tool by a Bangalore-based company leverages AI for task automation, time tracking, and communication streamlining.
- **Creately.com** offers AI-powered diagramming tools, including flowchart creation, with features like automatic shape

alignment, smart connectors, and real-time collaboration. It provides templates and customization options for various industries and use cases.

XIII

AI tools for Developers

The impact of AI on software developers is multifaceted and constantly evolving. While it may sometimes feel like AI is threatening to replace developers, the reality is that it's more likely to augment their skills and capabilities, leading to a more productive and creative development process. Here's a breakdown of the potential impacts:

Positive impacts:

- **Increased productivity and efficiency:** AI can automate repetitive tasks like code generation, testing, and debugging, freeing up developers to focus on more strategic and creative work. Imagine AI tools automatically generating boilerplate code, writing unit tests, or detecting potential bugs, saving developers valuable time and effort.
- **Improved code quality:** AI-powered tools can analyse code for potential errors, vulnerabilities, and inefficiencies, helping developers write cleaner, more maintainable code. Imagine using AI to identify potential security risks in your code or automatically suggest optimizations to improve performance.

- **Enhanced creativity and innovation:** AI can generate new ideas and code snippets, sparking creativity and helping developers explore new possibilities. Imagine using AI to brainstorm new design patterns, generate different user interface options, or even suggest potential features based on user data.
- **Personalized learning and skill development:** AI can tailor learning resources and recommendations to individual developers, helping them stay ahead of the curve in a rapidly evolving field. Imagine AI-powered platforms suggesting relevant tutorials, courses, or open-source projects based on your specific interests and skillset.

Potential challenges:

- **Bias and fairness:** AI algorithms are not immune to bias, and it's important to be aware of potential biases creeping into AI-generated code. Developers need to be critical of AI outputs and ensure they are fair and unbiased.
- **Job displacement:** While AI is unlikely to replace most software developers, some routine tasks may become automated, potentially leading to job displacement in specific areas.
- **Skills gap:** Developers may need to acquire new skills to work effectively with AI tools and interpret their outputs. This could involve learning about machine learning, data analysis, and ethical considerations of AI development.

Overall, AI is likely to have a positive impact on software developers, leading to increased productivity, improved code quality, and enhanced creativity. However, it's crucial for developers to be aware of the potential challenges and actively adapt their skills to thrive in this evolving landscape. By embracing the power of AI and using it responsibly, software developers can play a key role in building a more innovative and efficient future.

Code Completion and Assistance:

- **GitHub Copilot:** This AI tool, created by GitHub and OpenAI, helps developers by suggesting code completions, whole lines of code, and even entire functions. It learns from a massive dataset of code and can adapt to your coding style and preferences.
- **Tabnine:** Tabnine is an AI-powered code completion tool that can help developers write code faster and more efficiently. It can also suggest entire functions and variables, and it learns from your coding style to provide more relevant suggestions.
- **Kite:** Provides AI-powered code completion with function and variable suggestions, tailors to your style, and even generates documentation as you write.
- **Replit:** An online IDE with an AI assistant for code writing, debugging, and documentation, all within your browser.
- **Mutable.ai:** Offers context-aware code completion and error prevention, leveraging large language models to understand your code's intent and suggest relevant completions.
- **Polycoder:** Focused on specific programming tasks, Polycoder helps generate code for common functionalities like data processing, web scraping, and machine learning pipelines.
- **TensorFlow AutoML:** Designed for machine learning and data science tasks, TensorFlow AutoML simplifies model building by automatically generating code based on your chosen algorithm and dataset.

Code Analysis and Quality Improvement:

- **Tedax:** An agile data lake platform, developed by Tata Elxsi based on open-source principles, designed for the swift implementation and deployment of AI/ML solutions, prioritizing real-time performance and accuracy. A key feature of this platform is its ability to conduct root cause analysis of anomalous time series data, addressing a common challenge in application service monitoring systems.

- **DeepCode:** AI-powered static analysis tool that identifies bugs, security vulnerabilities, and code smells, promoting code quality.
- **Codota:** Another AI-powered code analysis tool, focusing on improving code quality by detecting bugs, vulnerabilities, and code smells, while suggesting style improvements for readability.
- **Mergix:** Employs AI for pull request reviews, highlighting potential issues like bugs, vulnerabilities, and code smells, along with readability suggestions.

Hugging Face: A Hub for Open-Source AI and Machine Learning

Hugging Face is a community-driven platform that serves as a vital hub for the open-source machine learning and artificial intelligence community. It offers a range of resources and tools, making it a valuable asset for developers, researchers, and anyone interested in exploring and using AI. Here's a breakdown of its key features:

1. Open-Source Machine Learning Models:

- Vast repository of over 120,000 pre-trained machine learning models, covering diverse tasks like text generation, translation, image classification, and more.
- Models are contributed by the community, ensuring a wide variety and catering to various needs.
- Easy access to explore, experiment, and integrate these models into your projects.

2. Dataset Hub:

- Hosts over 20,000 high-quality datasets for various machine learning tasks.

- Datasets are curated and organized, ensuring their quality and accessibility.
- Users can find, download, and contribute datasets, fostering collaboration and knowledge sharing.

3. Transformers Library:

- Open-source library for natural language processing (NLP) tasks.
- Provides efficient and easy-to-use tools for tasks like text classification, question answering, and summarization.
- Actively developed and maintained by the community, ensuring constant improvement.

4. Community and Collaboration:

- Hugging Face fosters a vibrant community of developers, researchers, and enthusiasts.
- Users can share code, discuss projects, and contribute to the platform's growth.
- Events, forums, and resources further enhance collaboration and knowledge exchange.

5. Education and Democratization:

- Hugging Face Academy offers tutorials, courses, and resources to learn and apply AI.
- Makes AI accessible to a wider audience, promoting understanding and responsible development.
- Democratizes access to AI tools and knowledge, empowering individuals and organizations.

Whether you're a seasoned developer or just starting your AI journey, Hugging Face offers valuable resources and opportunities to learn, create, and contribute.

XIV
Prompt Engineering

Imagine stepping up to an orchestra, baton in hand, and not knowing what music to play. That's what interacting with some AI models can feel like – overwhelming and unstructured. This is where prompt engineering comes in, acting as a teacher who guides the AI towards creating the desired outcome. In essence, prompt engineering is the art and science of crafting text instructions that tell an AI what you want it to do.

Components of a Good Prompt:

- **Clear Task:** What do you want the AI to accomplish? Is it generating text, translating languages, writing code, or something else? Be specific and unambiguous.
- **Context and Information:** Provide relevant information that helps the AI understand the task better. This could include data, examples, or specific details about the desired output.
- **Style and Tone:** Specify the desired style and tone of the output. Do you want it to be formal, informal, funny, serious, creative, or something else?
- **Constraints and Guidelines:** Set any limitations or boundaries you want the AI to adhere to. This could include avoiding certain topics, adhering to a specific format, or maintaining a certain level of factual accuracy.

Example of Prompt Engineering in Action,

Assume you're a movie director working on a Bollywood film set in Mumbai's bustling Chandni Chowk market. You want to create a vibrant and humorous scene showcasing the energy and chaos of the market, involving a street vendor haggling with a customer.

Here's a prompt you could use:

> "*Write a scene set in the heart of Mumbai's Chandni Chowk market, teeming with colour, noise, and people. A charismatic street vendor named Raju, known for his quick wit and persuasive charm, is trying to sell a beautiful silk scarf to a sceptical customer, Lata. They engage in a playful teasing, filled with colourful metaphors and exaggerated expressions, showcasing the art of haggling and the spirit of the market. Raju eventually charms Lata with his humour and knowledge of her needs, leading to a satisfying purchase and a shared laugh.*"

This prompt provides the AI with:

- **The task:** Write a scene.
- **Context and information:** Bollywood film, Chandni Chowk market, Mumbai, street vendor, haggling, colourful, humorous, playful banter, metaphors, expressions, satisfying purchase.
- **Character details:** Raju (charismatic, quick-witted, persuasive), Lata (sceptical).
- **Desired style:** Vibrant, energetic, humorous, capturing the essence of Mumbai and Bollywood.

With this information, the AI can generate a scene that feels authentically Indian and entertaining, filled with the characteristic humour and bartering spirit of the Chandni Chowk market. Try this prompt by yourself in ChatGPT or Google Gemini to understand the beauty of the scene.

Here are some other prompts you could use in different contexts:

- **For a historical drama:** "Write a scene set in the Mughal court, portraying a tense negotiation between two powerful emperors, using rich language and political intrigue."
- **For a social commentary film:** "Generate a dialogue between two friends from different socioeconomic backgrounds, highlighting the stark realities of caste and class in modern India."
- **For a documentary filmmaker:** "Craft a script for an interview with a renowned musician, exploring their creative journey and the influence of Indian classical music on their work."

Another prompt

> "*A photorealistic image of a South Asian woman in her late 20s with short black hair and glasses, wearing a professional blazer and dress pants, standing confidently in a modern computer lab. She is using a laptop connected to an AI workstation, her expression focused and determined as she interacts with the software. The lab is brightly lit with rows of computers and servers in the background.*"

Below are the results of testing this across 3 different models,

BlueWillow V5

Google imagen2

Stable Diffusion V2.1

Remember, prompt engineering is all about providing clear and specific instructions to guide the AI towards generating content that aligns with the desired context and audience. By incorporating relevant details, cultural nuances, and specific themes, we can create stories that resonate deeply with regional audiences. With a thoughtful approach and a touch of creativity, prompt engineering enables us to craft compelling narratives that captivate and engage readers across diverse backgrounds and interests.

XV

AI's Strengths in the Cyber Security

How AI is Turning the Tables on Cybercriminals

Cybersecurity is a constant battle against evolving threats, and Artificial Intelligence is emerging as a powerful tool in this fight, offering both tools for defence and presenting novel challenges. While some fear AI as a potential threat, the reality is that it can significantly enhance our ability to detect, prevent, and respond to cyberattacks

Let's explore the dynamic duo of AI and cybersecurity:

AI's Strengths in the Security Arena:

- **Analysing vast amounts of data:** AI can scan through massive datasets of network traffic, logs, and user behaviour to identify anomalies that might indicate potential attacks. This helps security teams identify threats faster and more accurately than traditional methods.
- **Predicting and preventing attacks:** AI can learn from past attacks and identify patterns to predict future threats. This allows security teams to take proactive measures and prevent attacks before they occur.

- **Automating threat detection and response:** AI-powered systems can automate routine tasks like analysing logs and responding to low-level threats, freeing up human analysts to focus on more complex issues.
- **Personalizing security measures:** AI can adapt security measures to individual users and devices, providing a more personalized and effective defence. This is especially useful in BYOD (Bring Your Own Device) environments.
- **Identifying and mitigating social engineering attacks:** AI can analyse communication patterns and identify suspicious behaviour that might indicate social engineering attempts, protecting users from falling victim to these scams.
- **Securing the Internet** of Things (IoT): AI can help manage the security of the rapidly growing number of connected devices in the IoT, identifying vulnerabilities and preventing unauthorized access.

Tailored Protection: AI Shields Crafted for Perfect Fit

AI personalizes security measures based on individual user behaviour and risk profiles. Imagine having a security shield that dynamically adjusts based on your specific needs. If you're a high-profile executive, your AI shield might be extra vigilant, monitoring suspicious activity more closely. Conversely, a low-risk user might have a more relaxed shield, allowing for smoother workflows. This personalized approach ensures optimal protection without unnecessary restrictions.

From Reactive to Proactive: Predicting the Next Move

Cybersecurity has traditionally been reactive(though not always), responding to attacks after they occur. AI, however, empowers a proactive approach. By learning from past attacks and analysing data from various sources, AI can predict future threats and vulnerabilities, anticipating the attacker's next move and enabling you to fortify your defences before the strike lands. This proactive approach can significantly reduce the impact of cyberattacks, saving businesses and individuals time, money, and reputational damage.

Challenges and Considerations: Navigating the Ethical Minefield

While AI's potential in cybersecurity is undeniable, ethical considerations cannot be ignored.

- **Data Bias & Fairness:** Biases present in training data can lead to discriminatory security measures or inaccurate threat detection. Imagine an AI system flagging a specific ethnicity as more likely to be a security risk – this is not only unethical but also demonstrably inaccurate. Ensuring fairness and transparency in AI development is crucial to maintain trust and prevent harmful consequences.
- **Explainability & Transparency:** Complex AI models can be opaque, making it difficult to understand how they arrived at a decision. This lack of transparency can hinder trust and accountability.
- **Potential for Misuse:** Like any powerful tool, AI can be misused for malicious purposes. It's crucial to have safeguards in place to prevent AI-powered cyberattacks.
- **Data privacy:** Training AI models requires large amounts of data, raising concerns about privacy. It's important to ensure that data is collected and used responsibly, respecting user privacy.
- **Human oversight:** AI should not replace human expertise in cybersecurity. Humans are still needed to interpret AI outputs, make critical decisions, and oversee the overall security strategy.

Overall, AI offers significant potential to improve cybersecurity, but it's important to use it responsibly and ethically. By combining the power of AI with human expertise, we can create a more secure and resilient digital world.

The integration of AI into cybersecurity will continue to evolve rapidly, shaping the future of both fields. As AI capabilities advance, we can expect even more sophisticated threat detection, proactive defence strategies, and personalized security solutions. AI will handle the heavy lifting – the data crunching, anomaly detection, and automated responses – while human expertise remains vital for strategic decision-making, ethical oversight, and navigating the complex social and legal implications of AI-powered security measures. This human-AI partnership will be the key to building an ever-evolving defence system, adapting to new threats and securing the digital landscape for generations to come.

XVI

Case Studies: AI in Cybersecurity

Here are a few examples of how AI is being used to combat cyber threats and enhance security testing:

1.Social Engineering Attack Prevention with AI:

- **Company:** Deepwatch
- **Challenge:** Identifying and mitigating social engineering attacks that target employees.
- **Solution:** Deepwatch's AI platform analyzes employee communication patterns and identifies suspicious behavior that could indicate they've fallen victim to a social engineering attack. This helped a retail company prevent fraudulent transactions initiated by employees tricked into giving away sensitive information.

2.Phishing Detection with Machine Learning:

- **Company:** Agari
- **Challenge:** Detecting sophisticated phishing emails that bypass traditional filters.

- **Solution:** Agari uses AI-powered machine learning to analyze email content, sender behavior, and network activity, identifying even subtle indicators of phishing attempts. This caught a sophisticated phishing campaign targeting executives, preventing significant financial losses.

3.Anomaly Detection in Networks:

- **Company**: MacAfee
- **Challenge:** Manually analyzing vast network traffic for malicious activity was time-consuming and prone to human error.
- **Solution:** MacAfee's DeepGuard leverages AI to analyze network traffic in real-time, detecting anomalies and identifying suspicious behavior patterns indicative of malware or cyberattacks, enabling faster response times.

4.Automated Penetration Testing with AI:

- **Company:** Tenable
- **Challenge:** Manually testing systems for vulnerabilities is time-consuming and incomplete.
- **Solution:** Tenable's Nessus platform uses AI to automate penetration testing, identifying potential vulnerabilities across complex IT environments. This AI-powered approach helped a financial institution discover and patch critical vulnerabilities before attackers could exploit them.

5.Malware Detection with Deep Learning:

- **Company:** Palo Alto Networks
- **Challenge:** Identifying new and unknown malware variants that traditional signature-based detection methods miss.
- **Solution:** Palo Alto Networks uses deep learning algorithms to analyse malware behaviour and identify malicious code, even if

it hasn't been seen before. This approach helped a government agency identify and block a zero-day attack targeting its critical infrastructure.

6.AI-powered Threat Hunting:

- **Company:** Palo Alto Networks
- **Challenge:** Identifying and responding to advanced threats hidden within vast security data was challenging.
- **Solution:** Palo Alto Networks' Cortex XSOAR uses AI to automate threat hunting tasks, analyzing data from various sources, identifying suspicious activity, and prioritizing high-risk threats for investigation, streamlining security operations.

7.Social Engineering Detection with AI:

- **Company:** ZeroFOX
- **Challenge:** Social engineering attacks targeting employees through email, social media, and other channels were difficult to detect.
- **Solution:** ZeroFOX's SaaS platform leverages AI to analyze communication patterns, language usage, and sender behavior, identifying fraudulent attempts at impersonation and social manipulation, protecting employees from these sophisticated attacks.

8.Preventing Ransomware Attacks with AI:

- **Company:** Blackbaud, a software provider for the non-profit sector.
- **Challenge:** Blackbaud faced a sophisticated ransomware attack that encrypted critical data across its systems.
- **Solution:** Blackbaud implemented CylancePROTECT, which uses AI to detect and block malicious activity in real-time. The AI identified the ransomware attempt early on, preventing

significant data loss and minimizing disruption to operations.

These are just a few examples of how AI is revolutionizing cybersecurity and security testing. As AI technology continues to evolve, its impact on this field will only become more significant, offering powerful tools to combat cyber threats and build a more secure digital future.

XVII

Case Studies: AI's Transformation of Media

The media landscape is undergoing a revolutionary shift, driven by artificial intelligence (AI). From crafting compelling stories to engaging audiences and navigating complex ethical considerations, AI is rapidly reshaping every aspect of the industry. Let's go deeper into its transformative impact through insightful case studies:

1.Content Creation:

- **Newsrooms Powered by AI:The Associated Press** leverages AI tools to generate routine reports and sports articles, freeing up journalists for deeper analysis and storytelling.
- **Personalization**: Platforms like **BBC News** and **The New York Times** use AI to curate personalized news feeds and content recommendations based on individual preferences.
- **Music:Spotify's Amper Music** creates personalized playlists and even composes original music based on your listening habits.
- **Times Internet**: Times Internet, one of India's leading digital media companies, utilizes AI-driven content creation tools to

automate the production of news articles and multimedia content across its platforms.

- **JioSaavn**: JioSaavn, one of India's largest music streaming platforms, employs AI-powered speech recognition and transcription technology to automate the transcription of audio content, including podcasts, interviews, and radio shows.

2.Content Distribution and Discovery:

- **Recommendations reinvented:Netflix**, **YouTube etc.** utilize AI algorithms to curate content recommendations based on your watch history and preferences.
- **Content Moderation:** Platforms like **Facebook** and **Twitter** use AI to detect and remove harmful content, ensuring a safer and more reliable online experience.
- **Targeted Ads :Facebook** and **Google** leverage AI for targeted advertising campaigns that deliver relevant ads to specific user segments based on demographics and online behaviour.

3.Image and Video Analysis:

- **InMobi**: InMobi, a leading Indian adtech company, leverages AI technology to enhance its image and video advertising solutions. By analyzing visual content and user engagement data, InMobi's AI-powered ad platforms deliver targeted and personalized ads to Indian consumers, optimizing ad relevance and effectiveness across mobile apps and websites. This approach helps advertisers reach their target audiences more effectively in the Indian market.
- **BARC India**: BARC India, the country's leading television audience measurement agency, utilizes AI-powered analytics tools to analyze TV viewership data and audience behavior patterns. By leveraging AI-driven audience insights, BARC India provides broadcasters, advertisers, and media agencies with valuable audience metrics and performance analytics, enabling

data-driven decision-making in content creation, scheduling, and advertising strategies tailored to the Indian television market.

4.Audience Engagement and Monetization:

- Chatbots: The Washington Post and The Guardian utilize chatbots powered by AI to answer reader questions and offer assistance.
- Social Media : Tools like Buzzsumo and Hootsuite leverage AI to optimize content and engagement strategies for social media platforms.
- Dynamic Pricing : Streaming services like Netflix and Spotify use AI to dynamically adjust subscription prices based on user behaviour and market trends.

As AI technology continues to evolve, its influence on the media landscape will only grow. From personalized content experiences to AI-powered news production, the possibilities are endless. By embracing AI responsibly and creatively, media organizations can unlock new avenues for storytelling, connect with audiences on a deeper level, and navigate the ever-changing media landscape with agility and foresight.

XVIII

Case Studies: AI in Manufacturing

Artificial intelligence (AI) is rapidly transforming the landscape of industries, bringing significant improvements in efficiency, productivity, and decision-making. Here are some prominent examples of how AI is being implemented in various aspects of the manufacturing process:

1. Predictive Maintenance:

AI algorithms analyze sensor data from equipment to predict potential failures before they occur. This enables proactive maintenance, minimizing downtime, reducing repair costs, and extending equipment lifespan.

- **GE Aviation:** Utilizes AI to analyze sensor data from jet engines, predicting potential failures and enabling proactive maintenance, reducing downtime and saving millions of dollars per engine.
- **Tata Motors:** Utilizes AI algorithms to analyze sensor data from their vehicles, predicting potential component failures and enabling proactive maintenance. This minimizes downtime, reduces repair costs, and extends vehicle lifespan.

- **L&T**: Employs AI-powered solutions to monitor industrial equipment in their factories, enabling predictive maintenance and preventing unplanned downtime.
- **Siemens:** Employs AI-powered solutions to monitor wind turbines, optimizing maintenance schedules and preventing costly breakdowns.

2. Quality Control and Inspection:

Machine vision systems powered by AI can inspect products with exceptional precision and speed, identifying defects and inconsistencies that might escape human eyes. This ensures consistent product quality and reduces the risk of defective products reaching customers. IRIS is an enterprise-grade computer vision and deep learning-based industrial analytics solution developed by Tata Elxsi. IRIS enables customers to deploy a wide range of use cases in factory settings, including quality inspection, safety compliance, productivity monitoring, and predictive maintenance.

- **Mahindra & Mahindra:** Implements AI-powered vision systems for quality control in their tractor production lines, identifying defects with high accuracy and ensuring consistent product quality.
- **Godrej Appliances:** Leverages AI-based image recognition for quality inspection in their refrigerator manufacturing, reducing human error and improving overall product quality.
- **Samsung:** Implements AI-based image recognition for quality control in smartphone production, ensuring consistent quality and reducing human error.

3. Process Optimization and Automation:

AI can analyze production data to identify bottlenecks and inefficiencies in the manufacturing process. This allows for process optimization, including adjustments to machine settings, resource allocation, and scheduling, leading to increased production output and reduced waste.

- **Toyota:** Uses AI to analyze production data in real-time, identifying bottlenecks and optimizing robot movements in their assembly lines, leading to increased efficiency and productivity.
- **Honeywell:** Deploys AI-powered systems to automate complex chemical manufacturing processes, improving consistency and reducing the risk of human error.
- **JSW Steel:** Deploys AI-powered systems to automate complex steel production processes, optimizing resource utilization and increasing production efficiency.

4. Robotics and Collaborative Automation:

AI-powered robots are increasingly deployed for tasks like welding, assembly, and material handling, improving efficiency, safety, and consistency in production lines. Collaborative robots work alongside human workers, assisting with repetitive tasks and enhancing overall productivity.

- **Bosch India:** Employs AI-powered robots for welding and assembly tasks in their automotive component manufacturing facilities, enhancing productivity and reducing reliance on manual labor.
- **TVS Motor Company:** Utilizes collaborative robots equipped with AI and vision capabilities to assist human workers in their assembly lines, improving safety and efficiency.
- **Foxconn:** Employs AI-powered robots for tasks like soldering and assembly in electronics manufacturing, increasing production speed and reducing reliance on manual labor.
- **Universal Robots:** Develops collaborative robots equipped with AI and vision capabilities, enabling them to safely work alongside human workers in various tasks.

5. Supply Chain Management:

AI algorithms can analyse historical data and real-time market conditions to optimize inventory management, logistics planning, and demand forecasting. This helps manufacturers maintain optimal stock levels, reduce lead times, and improve overall supply chain efficiency.

- **Hindustan Unilever Limited** :Implements AI-powered solutions to forecast demand for their consumer goods, optimize inventory management, and streamline logistics planning across their supply chain network.
- **Flipkart:** Uses AI to optimize delivery routes and logistics operations, ensuring timely and efficient delivery of products to customers.

6. Product Design and Development:

AI can be used to analyze vast amounts of data to inform product design decisions, optimize material usage, and even generate new product ideas. This can lead to faster development cycles, innovative product designs, and improved product performance.

- **Reliance Industries:** Utilizes AI to optimize material usage and design parameters in their petrochemical plants, leading to cost reduction and improved product quality.
- **Nike:** Employs AI to personalize shoe production based on individual customer preferences, offering mass customization options for color, materials, and fit.

These are just a few examples, and the potential applications of AI in industries are constantly evolving, driving significant improvements in efficiency, quality, and innovation across the entire value chain. As AI technology continues to advance, we can expect even more innovative and transformative applications to emerge, shaping the future of manufacturing.

XIX

Case Studies: AI Revolutionizing Healthcare

The healthcare landscape is undergoing a dynamic transformation, driven by the transformative power of Artificial Intelligence. From early disease detection to personalized treatment plans and remote patient monitoring, AI is impacting every facet of healthcare, offering solutions that address the unique challenges.

Below are a few case studies that demonstrate the vast potential of AI in revolutionizing healthcare.

1. Early Disease Detection & Diagnosis:

- **Niramai's AI-powered breast cancer screening**: This technology analyses thermal images to identify potential breast abnormalities, offering a non-invasive and affordable alternative to mammograms, especially crucial in rural areas lacking access to traditional methods.
- **SigTuple's Manthana platform:** This AI-based platform automates blood smear analysis, enabling faster and more accurate diagnosis of various diseases like malaria and dengue,

crucial in resource-constrained settings.

- **DeepTek's AI-powered chest X-ray analysis:** This platform detects tuberculosis (TB) and pneumonia with high accuracy, aiding in early diagnosis and treatment, particularly in regions with high TB prevalence.
- **Staar Surgical's AI-powered screening system:** This system utilizes deep learning to analyze retinal images and detect diabetic retinopathy at an early stage. It's designed for portability and ease of use, making it suitable for deployment in rural areas with limited access to specialized equipment.

2. Personalized Medicine & Treatment:

- **Apollo Hospitals' ProHealth program:** This AI-driven program analyses a patient's health data to predict potential risks for chronic diseases like diabetes and heart disease, enabling preventive measures and personalized treatment plans
- **Qure.ai's QXR platform:** This AI-powered platform analyzes chest X-rays with high accuracy to detect TB, including drug-resistant strains. It's currently being used in various Indian hospitals and public health programs, contributing to faster and more accurate diagnosis.
- **Genomics for Medicine India (GEM) project:** This initiative utilizes AI to analyze genetic data for personalized medicine approaches, paving the way for targeted treatment of various diseases based on individual genomic profiles.

3. Telemedicine & Remote Patient Monitoring:

- **Dozee's AI-powered contactless vital signs monitor:** This device measures a patient's heart rate, respiratory rate, and oxygen saturation remotely, enabling continuous monitoring and timely intervention for critical care patients.
- **Lybrate's AI-powered diabetes management platform:** This platform provides personalized coaching and feedback to

diabetic patients, remotely monitoring their health parameters and supporting medication adherence.

- **Arvī's AI-powered remote patient monitoring system:** This system utilizes AI to analyze data from wearable devices and medical sensors, providing real-time insights into patients' health and enabling proactive intervention by healthcare providers.

4. Mental Health Support & Therapy:

- **Woebot's AI chatbot in Hindi:** This chatbot provides cognitive behavioral therapy techniques in Hindi, offering mental health support in a culturally relevant language and addressing the language barrier for many Indians.
- **MindPeers' AI-powered mental health platform:** This platform connects users with mental health professionals and provides personalized support through therapy sessions and chatbots, addressing the shortage of mental healthcare professionals in India.
- **Sangath's AI-powered emotional support chatbot:** Targeted towards youth, this chatbot provides emotional support, information, and resources on various mental health topics. It creates a safe space for young people to express themselves and access help in a non-judgmental environment.

5. Public Health & Disease Surveillance:

- **The Indian Institute of Technology Bombay's AI-based COVID-19 prediction model:** This model helped predict the spread of the virus and allocate resources effectively, playing a crucial role in managing the pandemic.
- **NITI Aayog's AI-powered National Health Stack:** This platform aims to integrate healthcare data across the country, enabling better disease surveillance, outbreak detection, and public health interventions.

- **Pharmeasy's AI-powered medicine delivery platform:** This platform leverages AI to personalize medicine recommendations and predict drug shortages, ensuring efficient and timely delivery of essential medications.

Imagine AI-powered chatbots providing health education in local dialects, AI-driven diagnostics guiding treatment decisions in rural clinics, and virtual reality simulations revolutionizing medical education and training for healthcare professionals

MedLM, or Medical Language Model, is an advanced natural language processing (NLP) model tailored specifically for medical and healthcare-related text. It utilizes state-of-the-art deep learning techniques to understand and generate text relevant to the medical field. MedLM is trained on large datasets of medical literature, electronic health records, and other healthcare-related texts to achieve high accuracy and relevance in understanding medical terminology, diagnoses, treatments, and other healthcare concepts. Med-PaLM 2 is one of the text-based models developed by Google Research that powers MedLM, and was the first AI system to reach human expert level on answering US Medical Licensing Examination (USMLE)-style questions.

AWS offers a comprehensive platform for leveraging AI in healthcare, transforming patient care and the healthcare landscape.

Super AI

Super AI, also known as artificial superintelligence (ASI), is a hypothetical future stage of artificial intelligence where AI surpasses all human cognitive abilities, including reasoning, learning, and problem-solving. It's important to note that currently, super AI is purely theoretical and doesn't exist yet.

Key characteristics of super AI (hypothetical):

- **Surpasses human intelligence:** Super AI would be able to outperform humans in all aspects of intelligence, including understanding, learning, and applying knowledge.
- **Self-aware and conscious:** Some speculate that super AI might even develop self-awareness and consciousness, allowing it to understand its own existence and make decisions independently.
- **General intelligence:** Unlike today's AI, which is specialized in narrow tasks, super AI would possess general intelligence, capable of learning and adapting to any situation.

Potential benefits of super AI (hypothetical):

- **Solving complex problems:** Super AI could tackle challenges like climate change, poverty, and disease with unprecedented effectiveness.

- **Advancement in science and technology:** Super AI could accelerate scientific discoveries and technological advancements at an unimaginable pace.
- **Improved understanding of the universe:** Super AI could unlock secrets about the universe and human existence that are currently beyond our comprehension.

Potential risks of super AI (hypothetical):

- **Existential threat:** Some experts fear that super AI could become uncontrollable and pose an existential threat to humanity.
- **Economic and social disruption:** The widespread adoption of super AI could lead to massive job displacement and social upheaval.
- **Ethical concerns:** The development and use of super AI raises complex ethical questions about consciousness, responsibility, and control.

Current state of super AI:

While the concept of super AI is captivating, it's important to remember it's still purely theoretical. Researchers are making significant progress in AI, but we are nowhere near achieving super intelligence as depicted in science fiction

AI and Blockchain: A Powerful Combination Transforming Industries

Imagine a world where artificial intelligence (AI) and blockchain come together to create secure, transparent, and intelligent solutions. This isn't just a futuristic vision; it's already happening, with the potential to revolutionize various industries.

Blockchain is a distributed ledger technology that securely stores and verifies data across a network of computers, ensuring transparency and immutability.

Individually AI and Blockchain technologies are powerful. Together, they become even more transformative:

- **Enhanced Security and Transparency:**
  AI algorithms require vast amounts of data, raising concerns about data security and privacy. Blockchain's secure and transparent ledger system offers a trustworthy platform for storing and sharing data, addressing privacy concerns and ensuring data integrity.
- **Smarter Data Management:**
  Traditional data management is often isolated and inefficient, hindering AI development. Blockchain enables secure data sharing and access control, facilitating collaboration and enriching AI models with diverse datasets.
- **Decentralized AI Applications:**
  Centralized control of AI models raises concerns about fairness, accessibility, and potential bias. Blockchain can facilitate the development of decentralized AI models and marketplaces, promoting open participation, fairer access, and potentially mitigating bias.
- **Intelligent Automation with Smart Contracts:**
  Complex AI-driven processes may require human intervention, impacting efficiency. Blockchain's smart contracts, self-executing agreements triggered by specific conditions, can be integrated with AI algorithms. This enables intelligent automation, reducing human intervention and enhancing efficiency.
- **Real-World Applications:**
  IBM is collaborating on Medi Ledger, a blockchain platform that securely stores and shares patient medical data. AI algorithms can then analyse this data anonymously to identify disease outbreaks, predict patient outcomes, and personalize treatment plans. This empowers patients with control over their data while promoting medical research and innovation.

TradeLens, a blockchain platform developed by Maersk and IBM, uses AI to analyse trade data and predict potential delays or disruptions in global supply chains. This empowers financial institutions to offer better trade finance products and services, improving efficiency and risk management in the financial sector.

Wildlife Conservation Society is using AI to analyse aerial imagery and identify illegal poaching activities in protected areas. This data is then stored on a blockchain platform, ensuring its immutability and facilitating collaboration between different conservation organizations.

These are just a few examples, and the potential applications of AI and blockchain are constantly evolving. The potential benefits of this powerful combination are undeniable, paving the way for a future driven by secure, efficient, and intelligent solutions.

XXI

AI's Environmental Impact

A Double-Edged Sword

AI has the potential to revolutionize various aspects of our lives, including our relationship with the environment. However, its impact on the environment is multifaceted and requires careful consideration

Challenges and Negative Impacts:

- **High carbon footprint of training and running AI models:** Complex AI models require significant computational power, leading to high energy consumption and carbon emissions during training and operation. This can negate the potential environmental benefits if not addressed. Studies estimate that training a single large language model can generate as much carbon dioxide as five cars driving for their entire lifetime.
- **E-waste Generation:** As AI technology evolves rapidly, hardware becomes outdated quickly, contributing to the growing problem of electronic waste (e-waste). This waste often contains hazardous materials and requires proper disposal and recycling, which can pose environmental challenges.

- **Data Centre Expansion:** The growing need for data storage and processing to support AI development necessitates the construction of more data centres, which can have land-use and environmental impacts like water usage and cooling requirements.
- **Ethical Concerns:** AI algorithms can have unintended consequences, leading to environmental damage if not carefully designed and implemented. For example, AI-powered resource management might prioritize short-term efficiency over long-term sustainability.

XXII
Role of AI in Business Strategy

Artificial Intelligence (AI) has emerged as a transformative force in the business landscape, revolutionizing the way companies operate, compete, and innovate. As organizations navigate the complexities of the modern market, AI has become an indispensable tool in shaping business strategy and driving sustainable growth.

At the heart of AI's role in business strategy lies its ability to analyse vast amounts of data with unprecedented speed and accuracy. By leveraging machine learning algorithms and advanced analytics, companies can extract valuable insights from data streams, enabling informed decision-making and proactive strategic planning. From customer behaviour patterns to market trends and operational efficiencies, AI empowers organizations to harness the power of data-driven intelligence to stay ahead of the curve.

One of the key areas where AI has made a significant impact is in enhancing customer experience and engagement. Through personalized recommendations, predictive analytics, and natural language processing, businesses can deliver tailored offerings and seamless interactions, fostering stronger customer relationships and driving brand loyalty. Moreover, AI-powered chatbots and virtual assistants enable round-the-clock customer support, improving accessibility and responsiveness.

In addition to customer-centric applications, AI plays a pivotal role in optimizing internal operations and resource allocation. By automating repetitive tasks, streamlining workflows, and predicting maintenance needs, AI-powered systems enhance operational efficiency and drive cost savings. Furthermore, AI-driven predictive modelling enables organizations to forecast demand, manage inventory levels, and optimize supply chain logistics, ensuring timely delivery and minimizing disruptions.

Beyond operational enhancements, AI empowers organizations to unlock new opportunities for innovation and growth. Through predictive analytics and trend analysis, businesses can identify emerging market trends, capitalize on untapped market segments, and develop innovative products and services. Moreover, AI-driven research and development accelerate the pace of innovation, enabling companies to stay agile and responsive to evolving market demands.

However, as organizations embrace AI as a strategic enabler, they must also address critical considerations related to data privacy, security, and ethical implications. Ensuring the responsible and ethical use of AI requires robust governance frameworks, transparent practices, and ongoing monitoring to mitigate risks and safeguard against unintended consequences.

In conclusion, AI has become an integral component of modern business strategy, driving innovation, enhancing competitiveness, and enabling sustainable growth. By harnessing the power of AI-driven insights and capabilities, organizations can unlock new opportunities, optimize operations, and deliver unparalleled value to customers. As businesses continue to evolve in the digital age, embracing AI as a strategic imperative will be essential to staying ahead of the curve and achieving long-term success.

Wishing all Success

Nikhil Raj Natarajan

www.ingramcontent.com/pod-product-compliance
Ingram Content Group UK Ltd.
Pitfield, Milton Keynes, MK11 3LW, UK
UKHW042013190726
13854UKWH00005B/2271

9 798893 221749